THE PORTAGE POETRY SERIES

SERIES TITLES

Bowed As If Laden With Snow
Megan Wildhood

Silent Letter
Gail Hanlon

New Wilderness
Jenifer DeBellis

Fulgurite
Catherine Kyle

The Body Is Burden and Delight
Sharon White

Bone Country
Linda Nemec Foster

Not Just the Fire
R.B. Simon

Monarch
Heather Bourbeau

The Walk to Cefalù
Lynne Viti

The Found Object Imagines a Life: New and Selected Poems
Mary Catherine Harper

Naming the Ghost
Emily Hockaday

Mourning
Dokubo Melford Goodhead

Messengers of the Gods: New and Selected Poems
Kathryn Gahl

After the 8-Ball
Colleen Alles

Careful Cartography
Devon Bohm

Broken On the Wheel
Barbara Costas-Biggs

Sparks and Disperses
Cathleen Cohen

Holding My Selves Together: New and Selected Poems
Margaret Rozga

Lost and Found Departments
Heather Dubrow

Marginal Notes
Alfonso Brezmes

The Almost-Children
Cassondra Windwalker

Meditations of a Beast
Kristine Ong Muslim

"In *Forgive the Animal*, Sarah Pape's disarmingly beautiful new collection of poetry, we humans, and our collected experiences are allowed a fresh rebirth from the crotches of bewilderingly conjoined entities: fish scales and pigs' feet; a bag of citrus and the tantrums of gravity; death and a tattooed rabbit; a father's bygone hopscotch square glimpsed through the brine of amber and filth, memory and machine. What exhilarating suspensions Pape fashions! What unlikely ornaments are drowned in them, before being resurrected, a little kinked for the journey, sure, but brighter than before. Pape's poems testify to the kind of light that—if we dare to be loyal to that which it illuminates—can stretch itself into a strange halo— sometimes fragile, sometimes badass, ever the thing through which incantation can finally pass. What an earth-shattering and awesome book."

—MATTHEW GAVIN FRANK
author of *Flight of the Diamond Smugglers*

"I devoured these poems, much the way Sarah Pape's speakers often call for *more, more, more!* A stunning debut collection, *Forgive the Animal* brings us into a world both familiar and strange, occupied by love, disaster, desire, and—yes— forgiveness. We're all in this together, she tells us: 'Recovery is not singular. It is a collective act of reinvention, of integration. Every room we walk into, still we choose each other.' I'm grateful for the wisdom that emanates from this gorgeous book."

—BRENDA MILLER
author of *A Braided Heart: Essays on Writing and Form*

Forgive
the Animal

Poems   SARAH PAPE

CORNERSTONE PRESS
UNIVERSITY OF WISCONSIN-STEVENS POINT

Cornerstone Press, Stevens Point, Wisconsin 54481
Copyright © 2024 Sarah Pape
www.uwsp.edu/cornerstone

Printed in the United States of America by
Point Print and Design Studio, Stevens Point, Wisconsin

Library of Congress Control Number: 2024942455
ISBN: 978-1-960329-59-2

Cornerstone Press titles are produced in courses and internships offered by the
Department of English at the University of Wisconsin–Stevens Point.

DIRECTOR & PUBLISHER
Dr. Ross K. Tangedal

EXECUTIVE EDITORS
Jeff Snowbarger, Freesia McKee

EDITORIAL DIRECTOR
Ellie Atkinson

SENIOR EDITORS
Brett Hill, Grace Dahl

PRESS STAFF
Forrest Campbell, Carolyn Czerwinski, Elyse Edens, Allison Lange, Sophie
McPherson, Kylie Newton, Mattie Ruona, Ava Willett

For Rik and Sylvia, for finding our way.
And for those who were lost before they could.

Contents

III.

I.

When you look back it is still awful, / but also beautiful. Nothing is smooth. / The light is always rough.

—from "Dedication" by Jason Shinder

Kin

Believe me, we erupt from split roads
and waterways, from truck hitch

and rivet. Born under the upturned. Borrowed
from blackberries, bush-warm.

The earliest places scooped from placental
chicken shit, ghosts in the dust-riled hose spray.

I thought you might be home. Built from fish
scales and plucked dart boards, margarine,

National Geographic spines. Might've broke
your dollars for penny candy in brown paper,

rotisserie chicken, and pickled pig's feet.
Did you know the mud-skirted boards,

cracked heels, and softened blacktop?
Were you there snapping geranium stalks,

turning green thorns into scissors? Before
all of this, I had a daddy in corduroys,

hung over his arm, river-caught.
I circled like river sediment, shallow

in the pan till gold shone through. Maybe you
were born at the bottom of something too.

Forgive the Animal

In the emerald of late winter, the field is textured with chickweed, violets, plantain, calendula, mallow. The skeleton of a barn leans into its foundations and a tunnel of trees give view into everything that lies beyond them. Bundles of last season's dry remains diffuse the jeweled grasses where robins flap above their nests, revealing what's most precious below.

Each of us is born alone and set in the middle of this field. It is unknown who will find us and how they will care for our delicate body, or our mind, growing and reaching exponentially with each breath. There are so many nights you must survive before you can choose the tenor of night for yourself. So many meals to go hungry. And what if the wrong ones find you tucked inside the brambles of your beginning? The distance between those sharp branches and the end is so long.

When night comes, may you know a kiss to close your eyelids, a prayer to keep the demons beyond the threshold. Even if your imagination tells you a fire is coming and no one will survive. Even if something apart from fire takes it all away, may you know the comfort of a night unsullied by shadows and unbridled hands. And if you've been touched and no one is left to love you and tend what was harmed, remember the field and the way birds tore the wind and rode the ragged gusts to a place without hands.

Ars Poetica

Wild onions peek through wet earth.
Small organs gleam clean under
the calico's loving tongue.

Burn pile of back-lot tangles, leg
broken from the seat. I tell you this
backward, comfort at the threshold

before stepping out the back door.
Our first house. Yellow as a page aflame.
Brittle boards grimacing a perimeter.

Under corrugated plastic and soil,
the sagging animal pen, three lizards
refuge in the underneath.

Some places you can't find the bottom—
only remains. I drop into the dark dark,
try to pull the objects back up.

First Home

Sticky and small, I struggle free
from the highchair, discover the house
dark, animals and air, strange and quiet.
Every meal was cut with a dull knife.
Childhood formed over rectangles—
the rooms, the leather chair back,
linoleum's faint brick pattern repeating.
Brushes and bottles click behind
bathroom door. She readies to leave
and I yearn to follow her to work,
put my ear to her chest and listen to
her voice through her flesh, a comfort
from the deepest place in her, where
I once lived. Down the long hallway
and back to the perpetual kitchen,
she sets me on the countertop where
we baked exactly one loaf of bread
once, tore it open with our hands, hummed
each mouthful. I hold us here as I prepare
my dough each week, high above my hands
folding and kneading—the clatter of bowl
in sink, legs swinging, watching her—
mother's beauty a clean, bright shelter.

Sugar

Next door is where the yelling is born, where my first best friend exits the front door of the falling-down white house, crosses the azaleas, and crawls on her hands and knees over to my yard, where the plum tree is base and fortress, delicate branches we call *barbed wire,* and green fruit is not for eating, we are told, so we pick it and hold it in our mouths to test who can suck on the tart stone longer, then dare each other to bite, and we do, and after she brings Wonder Bread slathered with butter and white sugar to the fence, I say *more, please,* and she goes back to the white house. I wait a long time. I hear her door slam and watch her balance slices in each hand, jumping over the loose mounds of dirt, and later when the plums turn into gold globes of light, branches get heavy, fall over themselves, but two high ones lean into her yard, where I watch through my window as she and her sisters bring empty bowls, and fill them with the fruit, sweet juices fill their open mouths, skins between their crooked teeth—*My fruit,* I say against the window. *My tree.*

Foul Hook

He let me thread the eyelets, sort iridescent lures,
  slip sinkers, and jerkbait. Avocado boucle carpet
  and the chipped sill

where I watched him slip through the fences. Yes, uncap
  the fluorescent marshmallows (not for eating),
  wind monofilament and hold,

for a moment, a minnow from the sieve-topped bucket.
  He shows me how not to kill or touch eyes.
  He leaves before sunrise and returns

long after with rainbow, black, and bucketmouth trout woven
  on a simple strand. (I would only recognize him now
  if he had two arms raised

and gills open.) He spills guts into dirt, cats circling,
  clips the fish's frond tail, scrapes scales, leaves
  a dark stain on the tawny grass.

Once, at the creek edge, he tasked me with gathering hellgrammites
  and damselfly nymphs, their ghosted forms
  under rock, faint pools of water

forming as I revealed them. He stood slender on granite, casting out,
  reeling. The zip and gasp of Coors. He hooked me in the
  places his hands went wrong and pulls

the translucent strings tight like some wild net.

No Telling

Mother told me that Father
would've blown himself apart,

tremor in his calloused fingers,
if we revealed the neighbor's

touch. *Trust me,* she says, *it's better.*
She once came home late and he,

splayed deep in a blackout,
had a cocked rifle set crooked

between his legs. The harm near,
paralyzed as we were, by the threat—

shots made somewhere behind us and
the deafening silence of the afterward.

Father saunters in on soft loafers, hands
empty, and asks, *Where is she?* Our eyes

broken frames teetering with weight,
as the photographs slip out.

Ladder

White bark, a stand of birch stitched across the coverlet, amber rectangle of afternoon sun falls across the bent father-body. Our house cracks under the force of him broken. Fused to the mattress and orange scripted bottle—a long stutter of little yellow pills I would leave next to the volume dial. He fell thirty feet and lived to say, *more, more, more.* The moments between the ladder and the concrete were the mouths of one life breathing the shock of survival into the next.

Before the scalpel, before his torso was plastered ancient white, he swung me away from him into the kitchen, the faux brick walls. A dance, open and careless. Behind us, trout smoked in the pan and we devoured it. Salt, pepper. Crushed lemon rind.

What stayed the same: truck wheels ground on gravel, hot dog sandwiches on brown bread, the worn shadow of objects in denim, six-packs sweating through paper bags, the chorus of roosters calling him onto thread-thin path toward the neighbor's acre.

The quiet care by which he scrubbed red clay from the cleft of quartz, that is how I wanted to be known. Before he flew, I'm told I was loved in an obvious way. It might not matter now, the void grinding him flat, dope's hand sweeping the air of his presence. The wrong air when he baked mercury in the oven hoping what's left was gold. That empty space where I love him, just before the concrete meets bone.

First Specimen

Pin her through the mouth—
       a moth in a shadow box—

shoulders framed high
around the ears, fastened

to the bed, his silver armature

sharp in a numb place.
       Give a way, help her

remember how he separated
the wings and eased the metal

in like a corsage—
her slight throat, flowering.

Forgive the Animal

I'm trying to remember us. I am trying to forget us. To write this, I must do both.

I have to stay my hands, even in this moment, in order to keep them from writing those same unforgotten forgettings again. *Don't look*, my mother would say, holding her palms over my eyes, and I would allow this blindness, retreating into my imagination where the thing being hidden was so much more grotesque.

But memory, I think I understand, is like a broken plate. Picking up the shards, you assemble the fragments. Holding it up, it breaks again. You rebuild it with what's left. Each time you hold it up to inspection, it shatters, and eventually it doesn't resemble its original shape.

Addiction can be like this too. Returning to the point of origin. The pleasure a thousand times more pleasurable than merely being alive. And yet it never comes back together in that earliest way. It transforms and depletes until you are holding handfuls of shards.

Nothing and everything made sense about his addiction. It was literal, which is why I struggle to find apt metaphors. Why I keep getting sent back down the same neural pathways and find myself confused by the doubling—the Then alongside All the Joy That Came After. Thank god for the joy. It is a living wall I must climb to peer over. Most of the time I don't want to see what's back there.

And yet.

When We Were Very Happy

Red was patent leather, geranium
blossom, mother's lips, satin

camisole. Red burst along the levee,
father holding the sparkler, knuckles

split red with work blood. Plasmic
red in high heat—tomatoes, sliced

thick, salted. July burst berries,
two teeth marks along my rabbit's

broken neck. Wound's signature.
Red buckles crossed over blue tights.

Red cheeks after crying, fireworks loud,
sparked in the dry grass. Ruby erupts

over the bay, cheering surrounds us.
Eyes closed tight. My cheek, his shoulder.

Stranger Unnumbered

The thirteenth summer, Grandpa dropped me at the pier each day, a quarter in my cutoffs to call him back. Terrycloth rectangle under the micron of bikini bottom, the one Nonie warned would sing men to my body, her wheelchair clicking outside the dressing room, like a frantic code or bomb. When he announced himself, voice like voiceover, muscle shirt rolling across the tattoo's faint script, a vibration lit new. I turned for him, little spit of a girl basted in Bain de Soleil, while the kids beyond us swam in their clothes, mothers watching. *All I want is a kiss*, he said, each day leaving before me, his absence turning off the sun. Grandpa arrived in a maroon Buick swoop, stopping for soft serve before home. I wanted it so badly, pressed the white chill against my lips, opening slight and lost inside myself, this small plot of secrets where I offered a stranger unnumbered thoughts, imaginations—the cell where my father lived, the pages I lived in, boys whirling from me, a horde meaning desire. On the fifth day, he pulled a photo from his wallet, a woman peered out, *My girl*, he said, and I couldn't ask: daughter or lover? Either, I was jealous. It was next to the graffitied phone booth, salt air breath when his arms held me to the wall, *Are you really sixteen?* he evened up against me, his lips devouring my *No*, his acrid tongue stealing sweetness, my bold invention. They were right about me.

Stay

Our house and the bar, porch light and neon,
sister points to navigate Grand Avenue's mud
frontage. No wonder a man mistook our yard
for a bed, his roused and God-ful choruses echoing
over the winter shush into my bedroom. I considered
all the people beyond the fence and hinges. Maybe they
were looking for me. Another man
                              walked the long driveway between
our home and the next with a knife. Police said, *Stay
inside until its safe.* I'm still in there. Part of me is. Still
wandering into the grass while my parents are gone,
trying a lonely voice in my head, peeing behind trees
thinking, I could survive the night
                                        if they'd let me.
All these witnesses to my cautious nature.

Rabble Rouser

She and her mother smoked the same brand—
Virginia Slims, and on the crumbling back deck
I took a drag. I saw stars. Her name was the first half
of her mother's two best friends' names,
Sharon and Mary.

I picked her up in my mom's Taurus,
no license, from her grandma's trailer at
the edge of the edge. She was on prescription
medication for acne. She tried twice to OD on
Nona's insulin.

We drove around singing "Dream On." Clearly,
she'd been practicing. I think she was jealous
when I went to the psychiatric hospital with
so few warning signs and a boyfriend
who wrote long letters in pencil.

Her pinched fingers threaded the air as she belted
Sing with me, just for today, maybe tomorrow
her voice breaking with effort, smoke scribbling
our slow cruise through the fourteenth year,
not much further.

The Tattoo, or, Failed Petition to the Son of God

If time were a blurred window,
dirty glass to view all, you might

see her shape extend as she pulls
the kit from her closet shelf and kneel

in the margin of the room, faith's light
blinking dull and persistent. But time

isn't a window, so you must sit blind at
the worn neural path as she sets the ink,

a cotton ball, and razor blade on her
bedside table. If cells could remember

the wound before it was committed,
her fingernail practicing the two small

crescents she will carry for a lifetime,
you might whisper, *Don't mark this.*

But your cells stand dumb at the memory
as she cuts two perfect straight lines—

one down, one across, hatch marks fused
into meaning—"t"—the first letter

of her first love's name and maybe
something about Jesus, too. If prayer

were a condition for clemency, as she's
told behind the church curtain, she might

want to live on earth. Instead, she grinds ink
roughly into blood, heavenly black taking hold.

Light Names

Steel and hammer's blow. Liquid ore.
Same glint of Dad's vice after things harder pressed.

Grasp at the light. Thick motes through late amber panes.

Times he left, I stood with what he left unguarded.
Ruin something, find something,

a small self tells me, even now.
Once, he drew ten squares—hopscotch on a clean gray slab,

where I fetched all afternoon near him. I wanted darts

but too many machines stacked around us,
a machine-made night.

The quartz-lined windows, glittering veins.

I conjure him again, test whether I am crushed
or made elemental by force.

Apology From the Yellow Rotary Phone

My butter receiver, filthy in the middle
from your grip. Six-foot cord kinked from
sought privacy. You made me complicit,

breathing Color Me Badd lyrics through
the bottom, plans for where and when
sieved through the top. Mouthpiece dreams

and sins alike, emergency numbers
undisturbed, names hovering like a parent's
dinner you beg to leave. I couldn't follow

you to him or tell anyone to protect your
neck, your wrists—just a conduit, lump
of wires and loyal dial, always returning

to zero. I couldn't keep from happening
anything past your voice, your furtive aims.

Forgive the Animal

When we place our forgettings out of sight, new memories emerge.

For example, my father. I could say it makes me remember his addiction, but the truth is, I never saw it. Much in the same way I never saw my beloved's smoke, just felt the aftershocks. The earth shaking and subsequent ruin.

Tug at the blanket and the opposite edge folds back. My parents' coverlet, the olive green one with the stand of birch trees stitched along the bottom edge. What remains from this early memory is that blanket, a yellowed slice of light cutting past the mustard pull-down blinds, and how you had to turn sideways to get around both sides of the bed. I remember the double mirrored closet and the hem of my mother's slinky burgundy dress, but that's only because I've written about it before. As a place of comfort. A return to somewhere I hid.

Maybe it's true for all kids, but I sought out small spaces to tuck myself away. The closet. The other closet. A hollow inside a clump of bamboo. The pigeon coop. A pillow fort with the hide-a-bed pulled out. Maybe you know why I hid so much.

But I also liked to be out for all to see. Pretending to smoke candy cigarettes at the edge of our driveway. Picking wild onions in the back property in a romantic way. And when I was older, wanting to be discovered by some mysterious stranger. Notice me. Say the thing that would allow me to unwind myself from inside myself. See my secret.

Do I betray my hard-earned remembering when I turn away from the familiar places? I've said this truth out loud so many times, it no longer teaches me, yet shows my scar. By now, my body has sloughed off its cells at least two times over, but not these memories. They are fused like wire to a tree trunk.

Our growth is indelibly parallel. As if my survival were some durable object I could hold out and show someone—proof of life. Birch trees unfurling their bark. The wounds transform into faces, symbols, and perhaps, just the organism they are.

A Gardener's Guide to the End

The peony's white dress torn
under, pink and yellow heavy heads

break in deference to the unyielding
sun. What grows large, year after

year, buds springing up even
when uninvited? Cut past

the bloom, the berry crushed easily
between your teeth. When I'm

gone, you too, will disappear.
Remember who taught us

the names—lysimachia, monk's hood,
veronica, valerian—remember

who was there when the sky broke
like spring ice, some place you belonged

before you knew the names of places
or how green can come all at once.

II.

There was no relief from being / human and so I turned to stone / and now there's no relief / from being a stone.

—from "Oh, I'm a stone" by Diane Seuss

Half of Us

Our teen years lasted the length of
one summer night, chipped nail polish
bathed briefly in streetlights, wildfire
smoke trailed clenched fingers.

Were they azaleas, the foliage barely
covering us, as the men stopped their
trucks to yell, *I won't hurt you.*
You can come out now?

Those gnatted headlights, still.
There will always be men somewhere
behind us. With luck, you'll write
a poem about them,

about the night we got away. How fast
heat multiplies you. Dawn arrived, and half
of us were pregnant. Once the babies were born,
we were never young again.

Ruination Atlas

A shock of marigold nestles in
a toilet bowl, men on boy

bikes, corrugated shelters
sag with gravel,

two filthy shepherds, fur mudridden
and obscured

behind chain link, pace against the curve
of road. I am a daughter

of this terminal pastoral, camel-hide hills
turned black
with lightning, with lava rock.

There's south side, where my best friend's

mother was killed
for her pocketbook,
his house then burned to the ground.

We saved his cat, Tiger,
singed and hiding in a bush.

He vomited and shit as we drove
the backroads away. Who wouldn't

with these blind turns, and above,
a plateau branded with an O,

where many jumped and died and
some survived—both were legacies.

Pigeons

Deep coos in the roost. Skittering claws
in nesting boxes. Squabs screech hunger and

she stands, child-quiet, somewhere off to the side,
watching, afraid of cauliflowered beaks.

Nothing is wrong. Some things are just unbearably
textured. Singular and discomforting, unlike the iridescent

oil spill of male feathers, purpled rings around their
throats, the high-pitched air cutting under their wings

as they bead a circle of instinctual flight. She is pleased,
studying how sky's blue drain churns them. Unlike most,

always on their way home. They transform and spin,
tumbling toward her. Always returning to the cage.

How to Be Emerald Moth

Mimic the industry of Bee. Love
night. Take seven miles and
project the carnal scent of

duty. The lilac feast inside us.
You know only the imperative.
Command your mate to make

more of you. Break off your feelers,
your wings. Die like each thing
you've consumed. Like verbena.

Forgive the Animal

The professor says that losing your memory is the only guaranteed way to achieve long-term recovery. For example, people who've suffered massive strokes have come back to consciousness not remembering their drug use and, thus, are no longer dependent. Researchers have tried and failed to find drugs that diminish association in the same way, but it's nearly impossible to select for just the dependency without obliterating the rest.

X to the value of the memory. We return to something we loved, not because we love it, but because we remember loving it the first time.

I've told the story many times. How I loved him the first moment I saw him. A kind of attraction outside of my control or logic. Later, a few years into our marriage and parenthood, I'll take a Psychology of Marriage class where I learn a theory about love that will stay with me. You walk into a room of fifty people and you will find the exact person who will trigger all of your wounds. They will find you attractive for the same reason. Together you can play out a ritual of healing by prodding those hurt places, tending to them, and ultimately healing together with mutual trust and agreement.

Or, you can take something sharp and inelegant and make the wound bigger because you're not old enough or aware enough or still bleeding too much yourself to understand what else is possible. Once, during one of our many conversations about the addiction, the falling apart, the infidelities, I asked him why he thought all of it happened, and after a long silence, he said, *Sometimes I think we were just young.* For a moment, it felt like a kind of freedom to see all of it with such simplicity. The tangle of moral failures fell away in the face of *You just didn't know shit.*

The Roots

I.

Smell the deep funk of the orchard overwatered in high heat:
Walnut, almond, olive—rows stuttering in the periphery

between their two dark towns.

The men, given to taking things apart, showed him
the molten solder, a sense of wires.

Ten squares made the town that made him. Hers were green hills,
molars aching to taste the callous, the origin sweat.

He held a flag for crop dusters, running diagonal
to mark invisible lines. Whir of propeller bent him in half.

She tried hard, but couldn't imagine the tilled earth patterns
he traced over her stomach, finger wings hovering.

They thought themselves pure, felt the sun and poison rising up.

II.

He was the wheel, a stubborn round
she rode over one edge and jumped off the other.

He loved the machines. The ritual and smoke
it takes to leave and return. Some blueprints

get mistaken for contracts, but there in the margin,
floating across her burnt skin after being naked,

a transcribed devotion. The kindness of bandages
plucked like petals. Of bushes where she panted

under his hand. She misquoted combustion. He let her.

Babies

He played Solitaire, absently holding
my hand, as I pushed with the work ethic

of a young pelvis. Five days labor, then
on my feet, moments after we were undone

from each other. It rained in the night, unseasonably
wet after so many months of heat. You changed

the season and slept like a baguette in his arms.
That first day, he had to leave, sell used CDs

or get fired. Milk gushed through my wrong bra.
Never the correct garment. How does anyone know

what they'll need to go home? Those hours
we were barely two bodies. Each face appearing

in the doorframe, not him, until it was. I cried
when we left the hospital—this untethered world,

our child its newest pledge. He drove too fast,
but you slept through my gasps and reprimand.

Orphans Come to Witness Our Wedding

Vow to revise histories of filth
through each other's thin fingers,

as the uninvited guests shake
the equation from baby's toes.

Nineteen and twenty, not enough
to make a black knot at the neck,

or proper underwear to hold guts
apart from a vapor-white chiffon.

Two girls arrive barefoot to watch
the practice walk toward water,

under wisteria, over chestnut spines.
They come back the next day clean,

hold out cellophane roses, twisted
and pinked bundles in their hands.

In the Same Room

We hot boxed this room, shredded
the wallpaper with *fuck, fuck, fuck.*

There was a time bad news came
every day of the week, and we didn't

decide it was over. You blacked out
the windows and I changed the locks.

Those days we'd put six hits of ecstasy
on the credit card and wake with sore

jaws. I begged you to stop looking away.
The gravel was up to our necks in this

room. You kept going. This blaring place.
This room where two windows once opened

to light—where I held the hardest part of you,
thought I'd die if I lost it. There. There we are.

Forgive the Animal

Recover: to regain possession; to find again; to replace what was there before. A flock of pigeons circle the downtown square where a decade of new trees grow. The town still grieves the old square of trees. We laced our child hands together and strung around their trunks. Their roots, buried and rotted in ways we could not see. Replaced with man-made shapes, a chlorinated fountain, and a half-shell stage under which ruby cocoons shelter from the wet, then the heat. The flock circles and lands, circles and lands, wings cutting silence in a predictable shape.

When night comes again, everything soaked from the next historic storm, you might want to disappear, might want the relief of no thing.

We think ourselves sheltered, but we could, each of us, be torn asunder by the wrong constellation of despairs. Even in the Country of Too Much, of inherited land, fields, and weapons, generations can be ushered to concrete. This is our story too—precarity in a time of opulence, an epoch where one man's fortune could save us all. Born in the mall food court and we are starving, mistaking the failing speakers for the sound of our own hearts.

Certainly

I believe in the words—
like, *caterwaul* or *eglantine*—

that the sounds alone can save
me. *Calendula* and *borage*

bloom off the tongue without
care, without water. I know

I've hurt someone, that the nights
were late, roaming drunk

and alone, and then not. Regret
tumults in the gut. Sweetness

in the mouth is not sustenance.
I believe in the brain, and the light

rail carrying lies and truth equally.
When you are born to secrets,

you listen hard for clues about how
to be. Every second, hunching over

to hear your own mouth, asking
your own ear: *What?* If you think

something's wrong, I believe you.
I believe you were out wandering too.

One way to lose everything
is tell the truth. Say the words.

Upright, Tossed

Her right half arrived before her
left when the car toppled—hips

shoulders, neck, bent into the future
ache she'd know too well. Hours

before the pain body landed, she
groveled for more coke, kisses

stolen in the dank hallway. Hunger
is mistaken, come by naturally,

seeking anything else rotten
to love. They climbed out high,

built a lie together. They earn happiness
much later, chain between the upturned

car and another, pulled it up, tossed
the vial. Beyond the corner he took

fast and raging, death stands closer
since. They scraped the earth by inches,

a rope left gathered loosely in the road,
and walked into the next terrible story.

Other She

Never more loved or alone, Other She
put a glass passage between
                         your lips and you
          inhaled.

Then the dismantle and ark of broken
appliances—systems failure—you
                    might guess and be
                              part right.

Oh, that delicate gold chain you wore
My and Other She's taste so different
                    for the same man,
          same neck.

I will never forget the arrow of screwdriver
pointed toward gutter, the ghost
                    of your hand
                         holding it.

Not the first tool used against me. Memory
tolerates reinvention. I was good at being kept
                    from but not
          the knowing.

Forgive the Animal

I wonder if, in kind, my hypervigilance is a kind of dependency. A symptom of agonies, strung taut since before I had language. From extended, repetitive trauma the hippocampus shrinks and memories that would typically get filed away into long-term storage stay at the front, fresh and new as if they'd just happened. My memory filing system has a glitch. *Don't forget this. Never forget this*, it says, as if holding to the hardest moments will protect us from worse. But in the way he's recovered, I, the one who loves him, also desire recovery. To retire the trauma sentinel who stands guard of everything good.

In the same lecture, the professor says long-term recovery hinges on our ability to record over the VHS tape of our original memory, replacing isolation with community, despair with connection, dissolution of relationships with repair, and I remember how, as a child sitting cross-legged in front of the TV watching a recorded-over video, a ghost of the original image would sometimes cut through. A blip, a palimpsest, something indelibly marked onto the material would interrupt the new story.

For my part, I'm learning to exist within the strata of time, both nonlinear and recursive. To touch and acknowledge pained places without sacrificing joy to the binary of memory or erasure. Recovery is not singular. It is a collective act of reinvention, of integration. Every room we walk into, still, we choose each other.

Turntable

She allows herself a two-step under
the drum line's bass

where gyration plays through the crease
of funk bodies.

King and queen of the co-op
grind to the stage front;

a whimpering dog head peaks from behind her heart.

Parents, in their fused imaginations and
hardened heels,

once dreamed of Alaska,
what might grow in the permafrost.

By the time she could see,
they were already strangers

and she grew separate eyes for which to gather them.

To believe they were more, to know
they crossed limbs to make her—looked for her

in the others' tanned features,
she kicks up a never known truth in her dance:

what beguiles her backward
is the same rough pavement they rode

on a needle, carving her from a single rut.

III.

See how the first dark takes the city in its arms /
and carries it into what yesterday we called the future.

—from "Trapeze" by Deborah Digges

Lust, Invention

His Camaro was up to the wheel wells
in muck; they held hands, the stink

and diesel fumes of early love in all their
crumples. She blushed at the tow truck's

approach—headlights cut through the swarms.
They say they reconciled because they could

survive the apocalypse together. He vows
to learn how to make eyeglasses for her.

She will find the water, knit clothing from stalk.
Can you see them—stunned in the quiet of dead

engines? That night they were pulled from the black
mud. Before the humorless driver carried them

away, she divided herself over his lap, pressing hard
as mosquitoes covered their bare skin. Even then

it seemed too soon to know that they would pledge
themselves to the end of everything. There is

the orchard and the memory of the orchard, where
they held hands, waiting for the ruckus of years.

How to Be a Succulent

Get fat. Hold water
like a fleshy spendthrift.
Underground, swell

without audience, knowing
lack cannot kill you.
Invite the heat to touch

your thick petals, then send
up a stamen as thanks.
Learn to bloom without.

Forgive the Animal

What happens if you take the moral failure away from substance use and still reckon with the real damage resonating from it? From underneath it? It helps, in an abstract way, to imagine the drug entering the bloodstream, attaching itself to dopamine molecules, invading the synapse, and then blocking the passage back out. No way to regulate the flood of pleasure, just receiving again and again the warmth and light of a thousand mother's kisses. Your brain, locked in a room of decadence. You become a slave to finding that same door, but it doesn't exist anymore. Just the memory of the room.

X to the value of the memory of released suffering. Of unimaginable pleasure. Of the brain bathed in relief and light.

It also helps, in a less abstract way, to imagine him as a child. The naked toddler with only a cowboy hat sitting on his tricycle. The one his sister told me would use his allowance to buy everyone else candy. The one my best friend told me would carry something heavy up a hill without being asked. And even in the throes of addiction, on the precipice of our unraveling, was working at a friend's house, rebuilding and repairing. Some integral part of him yearned to fix things, to help, even when the other hand was destroying in darkness.

They Repair What Can Be Seen

His boots crush the cold-struck heirloom
tomato's pale pulp in the hay-striated mud,
following the path of chaos feathers.

She woke him today, *I fucked up. I left*

the cage door open. His long body unfolds
from sleep and into duty, reaches for jeans,
crocheted hat, *Raccoons?* A weeping coward

at the window she is, immersing her hands

in boiling suds as he searches for what she's
already found, crooked and wingless. She doesn't
see the body but for the bend in his arms; he lifts

the wrecked animal, places her gently

into a hole the woman cannot see. This guilt,
an ancient metronome in her gut,
rising in time with each meticulous shovel cut.

Only Child

I want to drive four hundred
miles and whisper my poems
into the crabgrass over my grandmother's
grave, hear her warn me
once more, *Don't get pregnant*,
as I tip her toward the faucet
to rinse shampoo from her forehead.
She was right to fear my fourteen-
year-old body, trading my bikini
for *The Tin Drum*. Today the world
is untenable without her.
When my tumor first arrived,
she spent her sleepless nights praying
against the invading armies in my ovary.
By the next sonogram, she was gone
and the dark matter doubled.
If I could, I'd tell her I was cut
in two, gave birth to a tangle of material,
and if inclined, could have another.
You're lucky to just have the one,
she would've said, tracing the sign of
the cross over my brow like a bullseye.

One Good Memory in a Drowned Forest

Then one day, as if taken twenty years to develop,
you see your father in the pile of driftwood,
so many white logs upon one another, they fill the photograph,

intricate geometry of gaunt wood and he, in the center,
blue-checked flannel discernible only because you are searching,
again, this last memory of coastal highway,

the dark gasp of oxygen as you drove through the redwood trunk,
raised then collapsed the mustard canvas tent,
pinched the bait as the hook eased through,

until you ended up here at another trestle-crowned beach,
where the river flows both ways to meet the tide,
opening and closing its freezing lips over your small toes,

up to the flax-dusted thighs you hug your arms around,
teetering at the apex of the warmed trunk beneath you,
because you were there too, in this rectangle of old forest,

across from Father, not really looking at him, but relaxed near,
two human creatures, held in gloss ink over cotton fiber, archive
holding us somewhere I could no longer feel or fear. Yet, know.

In Kindergarten, My Child
Teaches Me How to Knit

On pencils they looped the yarn from a pink skein
and with tongue-protruding concentration, tucked
the lead point up under the back strand, gathered

    the yarn over, and began again. Their hands
    over my hands, guided by long, pale fingers,
    a softness not unlike the small valley between

their infant nose and cheek I kissed and kissed
till their mouth opened in joy and surprise from
the presence and absence of my lips.

    They loved teaching me the logic of repeating knots,
    and I learned, sitting next to them in the long hours
    of bamboo clicks and irksome forgetting. Bright ropes

and rainbow pelts gathered in our laps. At our feet,
small creatures built from rows and stuffing. They never
looked at the strands, hands and brain tandem,

    so even if a stitch dropped, they didn't notice or care
    to see the dip and straddle in the next row. Whereas
    I couldn't take my eyes off the two points, slow and

precise, undoing a mistake before it could be committed
to the whole. I want to say something about the fiber here,
the way we're bound to the pattern, whether the one before

    us knew they were held to it or not. They taught me
    a knit stitch is an arrow, and purl, a noose—it all depends
    which way you loop, the shape made under your hands.

Estrangement

I take a beam, balance it across two weight-bearing
walls. Trim the doorway, and imagine you walking

through it. Stairs spiral, though the wrought iron rusts.
Panes cracked in every window. Each day,

I bring mercy to the labor of rebuilding. At night
the locks are stolen and the porch swing unhung.

Notice subfloor rot—mold blooming black in the joints.
There was a time you might've joined me here

with plans scribbled on receipts and your own broken
dwelling. This shelter, more uninhabitable with every

hammer swing. The foundation cracks from pressure
and time. Blame the failing materials I was given, told

to repair a place for you, Father, long before you've died.

Decades Sober

Patterns don't disappear, they fade.
Like the grass' five o'clock shadow

on the path you no longer walk,
you see the way but don't take it.

There is hope as long as there is life.
There are the damages. Both are good

when held up to the other possible
beginnings. When he came home,

he pulled weeds from the boxes,
and it looked like joy. Ecstasy born

from everything not death. Forgiveness
arrives daily, still, like a beloved stray

who lives between these years and
the others. Suppose it might always

need softness and milk before we sit
down to each other. The occasion—

these decades and riches found in being.
Hands scarred and aged and holding.

Bless the Cats

Bless the cats who arrived in your imagination
that fourth year, the orange and cream striped one

especially, her beanbag legs and soft middle hung over
your little forearm like a stole. And bless the strange

world of her and her compatriots, their cardboard
encampments, agendered love triangles, tiny pants

sewn from pajama sleeves, they kept you somewhere
beyond our late-night house and slamming doors.

This cat's gravelly voice, born in the back of your throat,
once announced over Instant Breakfast she'd stolen my car

the night before, drank whiskey at Duffy's, and played a few
games of pool. I imagine her in the smoke-blurred bar where

we took turns not being a mother or father, sidling up
to the expanse of green felt, no bigger than one of the pockets.

"Bullit, neat," she demands, confident and guttural, swilling
the amber inch of her last one before putting her embroidered

muzzle to the next. What did she see, this witness to our sins
and nightly permissions? What secrets passed through her

so you didn't have to know—our little child seemingly asleep
as each night fell like dirty laundry and warm quarters.

The People You Can't Talk About

Light flickers on from under the door,
a gash in the mostly dark. They wait for you
to remember and you do. Gut clenched,

turn the cold knob under your palm.
They blink their eyes, adjusting to the future
where you live, join you in the living

room for a long review of evidence.
It will never be okay, they remind,
that you started your period at the orgy.

Another pipes, *In the bushes in front
of the church? Remember that?* Probably
not. You don't get your anger unless

you hitch it to the flipped Bronco, the tossed
coke vial in the ivy. *You mattered very little*,
they repeat. *Own it*, they repeat. You scoot

them back into the dark where they settle in
until the next testimony. *I wish you'd taken
care of me*, you say to everyone

who didn't. Alone, the tape is still running,
spooling out around your happiness. Again,
you must learn to love the fuck-up.

Forgive the Animal

Once we imagined each other just-born. We believed we knew each other while stilled in the star sack of Life Not Yet/Life Maybe Never. Perhaps it is the imagination inviting one body to touch another after a great rupture. When we can make something larger and full of light—a place not yet lived into.

His mother straightened nails from rotten boards and sold them to live. He got clean in a jail cell, the name of our child thrumming in his chest. The child grieves and finds beauty in broken things and frames them together, a collage of remains. The right constellation of despairs.

In the dormant gray branches, spilling channels, and flooded backroads, cocooned and tented bodies in ruby bags embrace the edges of everything. Holding to the sidewalk. Holding to the underpass. Holding to the banks eroding after decades of drought. Vervain clings to the soil too, long after extraction, emerges unexpectedly between rose campion clumps many springs after.

Father holding you. Beloved holding you. You holding the child.

Pledge

I was good
for a long time
remediating bad
done early. Perhaps
I am finally
only good, not
held in thrall,
bent to what
dared me to go
so wrong.

Prayer for Thirteen

Never find yourself on your back, wool blanket scouring bare ass
as you try to see the meteor shower over their rocking shoulders.
Let the animals find you wandering. Don't believe the first or next
one who drives you up to the dam. Don't believe when they say they've never
done this before and can't help themselves. Be at the ready for wild
odds and seeds hitched in your socks. Maybe your bedroom window
is a portal to stronger arms. The moment you open your mouth
to another's warm smoke, the skin between you becomes something
new, your body an instrument you'll wring and plumb till the muscles
ache. Let the animals find your feet bare, walking through each schoolyard
you leave behind. Oh child, you have already lived longer than I without
the abandonment of each lovely cell; you were born, hope on my lips:

Let the world hold this one; right their steps
as they stumble into the darkness we were given.

Heights

He says to move the old wooden
ladders from the fence. No easy routes

in or out of the yard. He dreams many nights
of cops and retribution. He tells me over

coffee how he got away this time. So attuned,
I wake if he tosses more than once. He has

a scar on his left pec. Between nose and lip.
Just under his eye. I was never hit as a child.

I read the weaker heart sets itself to the stronger
cadence in a pair. I wrap my arm around his

chest, feel the beating against my palm. There
are times we jerk awake as if falling, tethered.

Loyalty

Every muddy day of childhood I slipped, two cold
earthen palms rising to meet me, as the goal post

horizon tipped. I still fall. Three times in Seattle.
Rolling luggage. Missing the stair. Into rivers.

In the snow, he laughed at my slow-motion descent,
and I cried all the way back to the car, still that muddy

girl with no centrifugal force to hold her. Disarmed,
a second self already righting on her hands and knees

while the first stands above. Could she disappear into
the space between the felled her and the former upright?

Was it the missed step from the curb, or slumped bag
of citrus cradled like a toddler over my arm—eyes trained,

foreseeing him on the other side of the square? Macerated
by my weight, blood orange runs the sun down my arms

as I look for him to pull me back. The next her is waiting
between. Gravity is loyal to itself and she follows.

After a Long Time Married
—a golden shovel after Margaret Atwood

I wake to your face, where you
end. At first, some things fit
riotously when drawn into
another. No smear or haunt of me
left to witness or answer back. Like
barbed wire held tight to a limb, a
tree, time and pressure hook
metal to wood, wood into
ceremonial singularity—an
inexorable bond. As the eye
makes meaning of light, a
crack in the anniversary vase, a fish
lives its remainder with the hook.
Your body, your you-ness, is an
invitation to harm, to open—
the only tool to hold you, my eye.

What If Knife

My hand gathers his beard like a bundle of lichen,
the tattoo I gave myself faded along the thumb's ridge.
I tattooed my rabbit's ear for 4H that same year, thirteen
and learning how to care for a life.
And, how to witness death. I would reach all the way
into the cage. It swallowed my arm, the wire cut
into a door shape, rough and toothed. At the end of
my hand—the rabbit's softness—stretched long,
an airy warmth. It was easier to touch him through
the diamond-shaped wire from the outside, the pressure
of his small body molding a mosaic pelt, stroke him
without disrupting his captivity. To touch in fragments.

He smiles into my hands when I say, *I don't want
you to love anyone but me after I die.* I come from people
who only love once. I am not proud of this.

Taught to find the rabbit's scruff, lift him by tender
skin, he kicked, flailed in the moments between the air
and my body, then tuck into the underside of my elbow.
I mistook the burrowing for affection, now released
from gravity's terror, *shh shh shh* into his thrumming side.

Once in the circle at Narc Anon, we were asked
to imagine our loved one's death. To practice it, feel it,
see it, would allow us freedom. In this dream, the worst
happened. There was no more What If or If Only knife
held against our hours and minutes. In the pinch of a cracked
plastic chair, under the fluorescent light's stutter, a heat
entered me, the way milk let down when I would hear
our baby's cry, blood coursing through my arms, uranium
bright, a luminous grief as toxic and rich as the ground
where I dug his imagined grave. Oh, what I lived through
to love him when he didn't want to live.

When the neighbor's dogs got loose and crossed
over to our yellowed half acre, I did not see the remains,
just the cage torn from its brackets. The next morning,
a knock at the door. The neighbor held out a paper bag.
I hope this helps, he said and walked back up the gravel
driveway. Inside, two baby rabbits, white scoops of fur
and four pink eyes blinking in the bag's darkness.
It wasn't the death I expected. So near and by the same
mouths that licked my hand through the chain link.

My petty dirt-bound ghost with her arms reaching
back. How could I die and not still be on earth loving
him? So close I can see my favorite pore, I hold his
face, ask, *Will you shave one day*, imagining the skin
beneath the graying brown frizzle, buried for decades
under a furred self, reiterated, separated from the face
he wore when we knew nothing but brightness. When I
dreamt him gone and maybe never woke entirely. Forgive me
this narrow place I've imagined us. He gets on his knees,
places one hand inside me, the other outside. Time reckons
this hour with our past and future deaths and we live.

Augusts

Neck stretched back and tipped slightly upside
down, two weeks earlier I looked for the Perseids,

their August arrival scattered in summer's deep
pockets. Now, warm gel glides over my throat,

the wand echolocating textures and margins across
a horizon not unlike the one we scanned for flares,

those long tails of light when sound leaps unbidden
from the mouth. When he says, *a pinch and a burn*

a pinch and a burn, I don't feel the next needle but
for some pressure and the jiggling of his hand as

he pulls up an anchor of cells. Something familiar here,
prone, vision fogged by the drumming pulse, neck

flushed with something outside itself, unseen hand
clutching at me, the unswallowable, the unwelcome,

the inarguable body. I imagine the little smears
of my flesh mashed across glass, stained, and launched

into the many hands it takes to deliver myself back.
What will they report? It's taken so long to see

myself with awe, to murmur and yowl over decades
of Augusts an exclamation, *A rupture in the darkness!*

How to Be Fireweed

Know me as bomb
weed, the color that arrives
after destruction

boreal brushstroke
on spiral stalks.
Announce the heat

with my entrance—
a whorl, a fuchsia capsule
growing from granite.

Forgive the Animal

If the moment comes in the long years of loneliness when you're offered a sip of stone and you recognize the weight in your veins as a mother's palm, you are loved. If you mistake crystalline fractures for being adored and breathe their vapor, if you open your arms, your hands, your toes to the needle, if you tap the absence you can't forget and only ash falls from the bowl, you are loved.

If you mistake the field as a freeway underpass, as an alley, ditch, cardboard mattress, plastic blanket, your own carved arms, and wake to find your fingers black with cold, you are loved. If you recall only half the path back, the field never disappears. A wide-open space where sunlight pours over every surface lives inside of you. Above, the small, almost weightless bird alights on the tallest branch and looks as far as any eye can measure. Inside you, the field's horizon is infinite. Below you, networks of microscopic threads sing. Their song holds every part, every touch, every darkness, every joy. There is no burden the earth can't carry. This earth is inside of you.

And even if the ones who found you could not see the rare shape of your existence, contorted you to their own troubled inheritance, even if you were raised in the company of no one with only loneliness to name you, others can bring you back. You are welcome back.

ACKNOWLEDGMENTS

Many thanks to the editors of the following publications in which these works or earlier versions of them previously appeared: *Adirondack Review, American Journal of Poetry, Crab Orchard Review, Diagram, Hayden's Ferry Review, JMWW, Los Angeles Review, New England Review, The Pinch, Prick of the Spindle, Smartish Pace, Split Lip Magazine, Superstition Review, Thrush,* and *Under a Warm Green Linden.* In the long arc of writing and revising this book, the early and ongoing support of these editors kept me writing and imagining toward this collection.

Gratitude to the Vermont Studio Center, InCahoots, Storyknife, and Community of Writers for offering life-altering time away to focus solely on generating new work, revision, and reading deeply. In these spaces, I've found true community that has sustained me for years.

Thank you to the Cornerstone Press editors who worked on this book, particularly Grace Dahl, and to publisher and director Dr. Ross K. Tangedal.

My evergreen appreciation to my teachers, fellow writers, and mentors who have supported this work, making space for the grief and grace equally: Jeanne Clark, Mark Haunschild, Nate Millard, Mark Hall, Lia Purpura, Rick Barot, Peggy Shumaker, Brenda Miller, Nicole Stellon O'Donnell, Jose Antonio Rodriguez, Hilary Tellesen, Rae Gouirand, Marta Shaffer, Jo Hooste, Ashley Roach, Patricia Murphy, Pete Miller, Robert Krut, Matthew Gavin Frank, Douglas Jones, and Elizabyth Hiscox.

From the earliest poetic thoughts I put to paper, my family has encouraged and supported me to continue. For my mother and brother—together, we've found light on the other side. Thanks to my aunt Maria, who first modeled an artist's life. For my grandparents, who surrounded me with love and protection. Finding my grandfather's photo in his archive of slides that now lives on the cover of this book feels like a sweet collaboration beyond life.

I hold deep respect and gratitude for the therapists and guides who have helped me understand substance use disorder apart from our cultural narrative. The work of Gabor Maté, especially. And for my dear friend, Kim Jaxon, and her son Nick, whose love and sorrow live in this book too.

To my beloved Sylvia, the curiosity, persistence, and belief in process you bring to your art practice inspires me daily. The ways you seek wonder and reconciliation in the world are a gift to witness. Thank you for being the best reader of my poems.

Rik, the story of our lives—both the catastrophes and the mending—are far more beautiful and complex than any book could hold. Thank you for always saying yes to joy and asking me to join you there.

SARAH PAPE's award-winning poetry and prose have appeared in *The New York Times, New England Review, Fourth Genre, Ecotone, Crab Orchard Review, DIAGRAM, Passages North, The Superstition Review,* and many others. She teaches literary editing, publishing, and creative writing at California State University, Chico.